THE MICROWAVE LIBRARY

C O O K I N G   W I T H

Pasta

ELIZABETH CORNISH

THE MICROWAVE LIBRARY

COOKING WITH

Pasta

ELIZABETH CORNISH

the apple press

A QUINTET BOOK

Published by Apple Press Ltd
293 Gray's Inn Road
London WC1X 8QF

ISBN 1-85076-095-0

This book was designed and produced by
Quintet Publishing Limited
6 Blundell Street
London N7 9BH

Art Director: Peter Bridgewater
Photographers: Michael Bull and Trevor Wood
Home Economist: Veronica Bull
Typeset in Great Britain by
Central Southern Typesetters, Eastbourne
Manufactured in Hong Kong by Regent
Publishing Services Limited
Printed in Hong Kong by Leefung-Asco Printers
Limited

CONTENTS

PASTA

THE Italians claim to have as many types of pasta as there are days of the year, and when it comes to sauces their imagination never flags. Apart from the meat ragù traditionally served in Bologna, there are sauces of prawns, spinach, clams, chicken livers, herbs, tuna, beans, asparagus, cheese, squid, garlic, cream, mushrooms and even chillies (chilis), nuts and raisins.

Cooking with a microwave brings all these delicious flavours of Italy to your table with less fuss than ever before. If you have had problems with overcooked pasta sticking together in a lump, a kitchen full of steam and a saucepan that needs soaking for a week, relax: your microwave will come to the rescue. You can cook and serve pasta in the same dish, heating up the sauce while the pasta rests until it is just perfectly *al dente*.

Pasta is traditionally served in Italy as a starter, which is probably why it has unfairly been called fattening. A pasta dish from this book followed by a meat or fish dish with vegetables, then cheese and fruit would certainly be a very calorific meal. But the same pasta dish with a crisp salad and a glass of wine is a healthy balanced meal, and won't make you fat. Many of the sauces in this book are low-calorie anyway, because microwave cooking needs little or no fat.

Pasta should always have a little bit of a bite left in it (*al dente* = 'to the tooth') and it should always be served very hot in hot soup plates; offer extra black pepper and Parmesan cheese at the table. Cheese is not served on fish dishes in Italy.

When you are making an olive oil dressing for pasta (or for a salad too, for that matter), use the best olive oil you can afford. *Extra vergine* is the golden green oil from the first cold pressing, and it is both pungent and delicious.

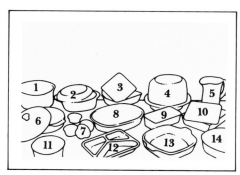

A selection of cookware, some of it specially designed for the microwave oven, which is suitable for microwaving.

1 Thorpak cake dish **2** Thorpak casserole dish **3** Microware freezer dishes **4** Roasting dish **5** Thorpak jug **6** Browning dish **7** Minidishes (ramekins) **8** Double microwave serving dish **9** Glass loaf pan **10** Glass casserole with lid **11** Cake or soufflé dish **12** Three-section vegetable dish **13** Browning dish **14** Glass ovenproof dish

ABOUT THE MICROWAVE OVEN

IF YOU are new to cooking with the microwave, the first thing to do is to read the instruction booklet supplied with your model. This will tell you all you need to know about how your cooker works and how to operate it.

Microwave cookers work by emitting concentrated infra red radiation that penetrates and therefore heats food much faster than conventional cookers. They consequently save considerably on cooking time.

The microwave is like any other kitchen appliance that makes life easier for the cook. Once you are used to it, which takes remarkably little time for such a sophisticated gadget, experience will tell you how long it will take to cook or reheat a given dish. If in doubt, always undercook – you can easily add on another minute or so.

To familiarize yourself with the cooker try baking a potato. Scrub the potato and prick the skin a few times with a fork. Lay it on a piece of absorbent kitchen paper and cook on full power for about 6 minutes for a 175 g/6 oz potato. Stop cooking half-way through to turn the potato over. A successfully baked potato will demonstrate how easy microwave cooking is.

Remember to stir or rearrange items during cooking or the food may not be evenly cooked, and

always cover a dish with a lid or cling film (plastic wrap) which you have pierced in two or three places with a knife to make vents through which the steam can escape.

Don't use anything metallic in the microwave, and this includes china decorated with silver or gold leaf. If you want to test if a dish is microwave-proof, put it in the oven next to a cup of water and cook on full for a minute. If the water is hot and the dish stays cool, it is safe to use. If the dish is hotter than the water, avoid using it.

Always prick the skins of vegetables and fish to prevent them from bursting. Eggs should always be pricked for the same reason. Never put an egg in its shell in the microwave – it will explode.

Where the recipe times in this book are not specific, this is to avoid errors. A microwave may be a scientific instrument, but neither cooks nor food can be standardized. No two carrots are the same shape and no two cooks cut them up in the same way. It is *always* safer to undercook and test.

Crockery, cutlery (flatware, glassware and cookware such as this must NOT be used in a microwave oven.

1 Ceramics with metal decoration **2** Dishes with metal decoration and glazes containing metal **3** Cutlery (silverware or flatware) **4** Metal flan tin and disposable foil bakeware **5** Glassware with metal rim or bands **6** Metal pots and pans **7** Metal bakeware **8** Metal skewers or fondue forks

TAGLIATELLE WITH VEGETABLES AND HAM

SERVES 4 / SET: FULL

Ingredients

15 ml/1 tbsp olive oil
1 clove garlic, crushed (minced)
1 small onion, chopped
2 courgettes (zucchini), chopped
1 small red pepper, diced
1¼ cups/100 g/4 oz mushrooms, wiped and sliced
⅓ cup/50 g/2 oz ham, chopped
¾ cup/200 g/7 oz tinned (canned) tomatoes, drained and mashed
salt and freshly ground black pepper
400 g/14 oz tagliatelle
boiling water
chopped parsley
Parmesan cheese

◆ Put the oil in a bowl and cook for 30 seconds. Add the garlic and onion and cook for 2 minutes. Add the courgettes (zucchini), red pepper and mushrooms, cover with vented cling wrap (plastic wrap) and cook for 3 minutes. Add the ham and tomatoes, cover and cook for 2 minutes. Season to taste. Keep warm.

◆ Put the tagliatelle in a deep pot, just cover with boiling water and add a pinch of salt and a few drops of oil. Cover and cook for 6 minutes. Let the pot stand, covered, while you reheat the sauce if necessary.

◆ Drain the pasta, pour on the sauce, sprinkle with parsley and serve with plenty of Parmesan cheese.

PASTA WITH EARLY SUMMER VEGETABLES

SERVES 4 / SET: FULL

Ingredients

400 g/14 oz tagliatelle
boiling water
salt
oil
2/3 cup/100 g/4 oz broad (java) beans (shelled weight)
1 cup/100 g/4 oz peas
1 cup/100 g/4 oz green beans, topped and tailed (trimmed) and cut into pieces
2/3 cup/150 ml/1/4 pt single (light) cream
chopped fresh herbs
Parmesan cheese
freshly ground black pepper

◆ Put the tagliatelle in a deep pot and just cover with boiling water. Add a pinch of salt and a few drops of oil, cover and cook for 6 minutes. Set aside, covered.

◆ Put the broad (java) beans, peas and green beans in a bowl with the cream. Cover with vented cling wrap (plastic wrap) and cook for 3 minutes.

◆ Drain the pasta, pour over the vegetable mixture and sprinkle with chopped fresh herbs.

◆ Serve hot with Parmesan cheese and offer black pepper at the table.

PENNE WITH SULTANAS (WHITE RAISINS) AND PINE NUTS

SERVES 4 / SET: FULL

Ingredients

3½ cups/400 g/14 oz penne (pasta quills)

boiling water

salt

45 ml/3 tbsp olive oil

1 clove garlic, chopped

3 tbsp/40 g/1½ oz sultanas (white raisins), plumped up in a little marsala

¼ cup/40 g/1½ oz pine nuts

45 ml/3 tbsp finely chopped fennel leaves

grated Parmesan cheese

freshly ground black pepper

◆ Put the penne in a bowl and pour on enough boiling water to cover. Add a pinch of salt and a few drops of oil, cover and cook for 9 minutes. Set aside, covered, while you prepare the sauce.

◆ Put the olive oil in a dish and cook for 30 seconds. Add the garlic and cook for 1 minute. Stir in the sultanas (white raisins) and pine nuts and cook for 2 minutes, stirring once.

◆ Drain the pasta, pour on the sauce, add the fennel and toss well.

◆ Serve with plenty of freshly grated Parmesan cheese and offer black pepper at the table.

RIGATONI WITH BORLOTTI BEANS

SERVES 4 / SET: FULL

Ingredients

3½ cups/400 g/14 oz rigatoni (or macaroni)

boiling water

salt

30 ml/2 tbsp olive oil

2 tbsp/25 g/1 oz butter

1 clove garlic, crushed (minced)

400 g/14 oz can borlotti beans, drained

1½ cups/175 g/6 oz mozzarella cheese, diced

chopped parsley

freshly ground black pepper

◆ Put the pasta in a deep pot and pour over enough boiling water to just cover. Add a pinch of salt and a few drops of the oil, cover and cook for 10 minutes. Leave covered.

◆ Put the remaining oil in a bowl with the butter and cook for 1 minute. Add the garlic and cook for 1 minute. Stir in the borlotti beans and cook for 2 minutes.

◆ Drain the pasta and stir in the bean mixture and cheese. Cover and cook for 1½ minutes, until the mozzarella begins to melt.

◆ Sprinkle with chopped parsley and serve. Offer black pepper at the table.

Rigatoni with Borlotti beans

SPAGHETTI WITH RICOTTA AND ALMONDS

SERVES 4 / SET: FULL AND MEDIUM

Ingredients

400 g/14 oz spaghetti
4½ cups/1 l/1¾ pt boiling water (approx.)
salt
oil
¾ cup/75 g/3 oz ground almonds
⅔ cup/100 g/4 oz ricotta cheese
150 ml/¼ pt single (light) cream
a pinch of mixed (sweet baking) spice
flaked (slivered) toasted almonds
Parmesan cheese

A delicious and very unusual combination of tastes.

◆ Hold the spaghetti in a deep pot and pour the water over it. As it softens, push the spaghetti under the water. Add a pinch of salt and a few drops of oil, cover and cook on full power for 12 minutes. Let the pot stand, covered, while you make the sauce.

◆ Blend together the ground almonds, ricotta cheese and cream. Stir in the mixed (sweet baking) spice to taste. Cover and heat through on medium power for 3 minutes.

◆ Drain the pasta and stir in the sauce.

◆ Sprinkle with flaked (slivered) toasted almonds and serve hot with plenty of Parmesan cheese.

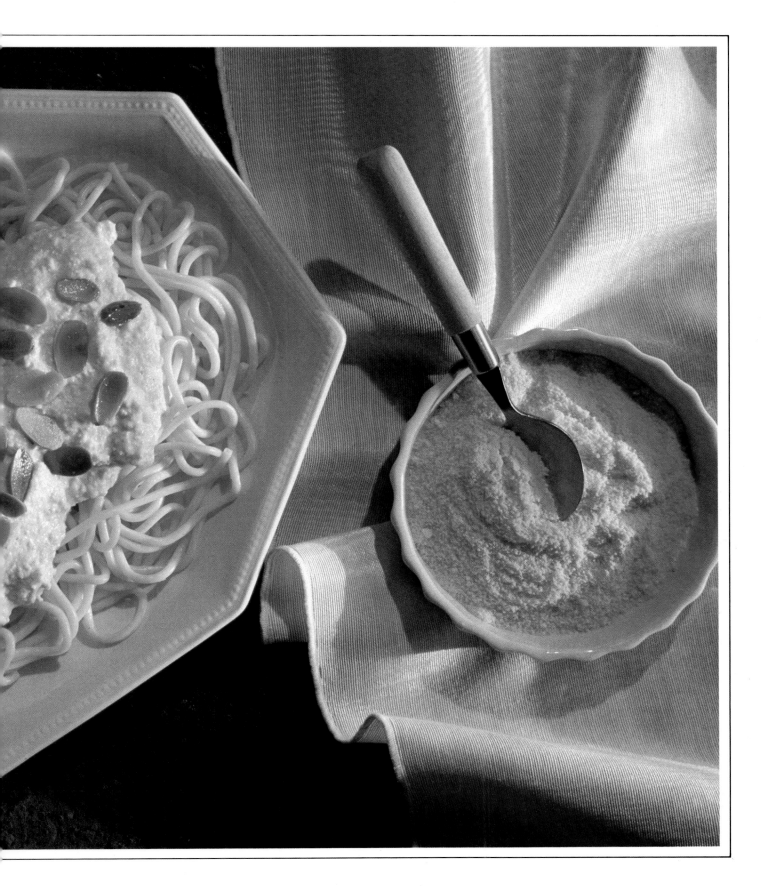

PENNE WITH COURGETTES (ZUCCHINI) AND PISTACHIO NUTS

SERVES 4 / SET: FULL

Ingredients

3½ cups/400 g/14 oz penne (pasta quills)
salt
30–45 ml/2–3 tbsp olive oil
2½ cups/300 g/10 oz baby courgettes (zucchini), sliced
30 ml/2 tbsp water
1 clove garlic, crushed (minced)
⅓ cup/50 g/2 oz pistachio nuts, shelled
freshly ground black pepper
Parmesan cheese (optional)

◆ Put the penne in a deep pot and just cover with boiling water. Add a pinch of salt and a few drops of the oil, cover and cook for 9 minutes. Set aside, covered.

◆ Put the courgettes (zucchini) in a dish with the water, cover with vented cling wrap (plastic wrap) and cook for 3 minutes.

◆ Put the olive oil in a dish and cook for 30 seconds. Add the garlic and cook for 1 minute. Drain the courgettes and add them with the pistachio nuts. Stir well to coat in the oil. Cover and cook for 1–2 minutes.

◆ Drain the pasta, pour over the sauce and season with black pepper. Offer Parmesan cheese at the table, if liked.

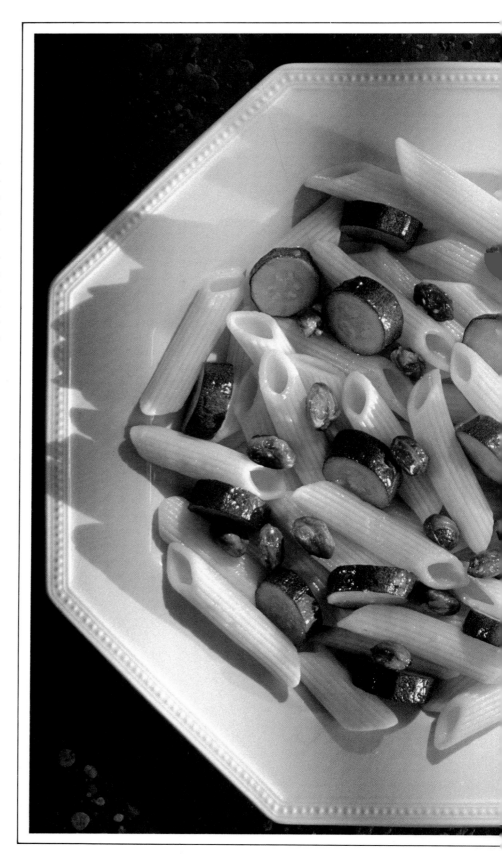

Penne with courgettes (zucchini) and pistachio nuts.

SPAGHETTI WITH AUBERGINES (EGG-PLANT) AND GARLIC

SERVES 4 / SET: FULL

Ingredients
400 g/14 oz spaghetti
4½ cups/1 l/1¾ pt boiling water
1 large aubergine (eggplant)
30–45 ml/2–3 tbsp olive oil
1–2 cloves garlic, crushed (minced)
Parmesan cheese (optional)

◆ Hold the spaghetti in a pot and pour on the boiling water. Push the spaghetti into it, add a few drops of oil and a little salt. Cover and cook for 12 minutes.
◆ Meanwhile, top and tail (trim) the aubergine (eggplant) and cut into thick matchsticks.
◆ Remove the spaghetti from the microwave when it is ready and leave to stand, covered.
◆ Put the olive oil in a dish and add the garlic and aubergine. Cover and cook for 5 minutes, stirring once.
◆ Drain the spaghetti and toss in the aubergine and garlic.
◆ Serve with Parmesan cheese if liked.

SPAGHETTI WITH GARLIC AND OIL

SERVES 4 / SET: FULL

Ingredients

400 g/14 oz spaghetti
4½ cups/1 l/1¾ pt boiling water
salt
45 ml/3 tbsp olive oil
2 cloves of garlic, crushed (minced)
freshly ground black pepper

◆ Hold the spaghetti in a pot and pour on the boiling water. Push the spaghetti down into the water, add a pinch of salt and a few drops of oil, cover and cook for 12 minutes. Leave to stand, covered, while you prepare the sauce.
◆ Put the oil in a bowl and cook for 45 seconds. Add the garlic and cook for 2–3 minutes.
◆ Drain the spaghetti, pour over the hot garlic oil, add pepper, toss well and serve immediately.

MACARONI WITH TUNA FISH

SERVES 4 / SET: FULL

Ingredients

3 tbsp/40 g/1½ oz butter
6 tbsp/40 g/1½ oz flour
1¼ cups/300 ml/½ pt milk
4½ tbsp/40 g/1½ oz Parmesan cheese
salt and pepper
3½ cups/400 g/14 oz macaroni
boiling water
oil
1 scant cut/200 g/7 oz tinned (canned) tuna in brine, drained and flaked
pepper slices to garnish

◆ First make the sauce. Put the butter in a bowl and cook for 1 minute. Stir in the flour and cook for 1 minute. Stir in the milk and cook for 3 minutes, whisking after each minute. Stir in the cheese and cook for 1 minute. Whisk again and season to taste. Keep warm.
◆ Put the macaroni in a deep pot and just cover with boiling water. Add a pinch of salt and a few drops of oil. Cover and cook for 10 minutes. Let the pot stand, covered, for 3 minutes.
◆ Drain the pasta, stir in the sauce and tuna fish and heat through for 2–3 minutes. Garnish with pepper slices and serve hot.

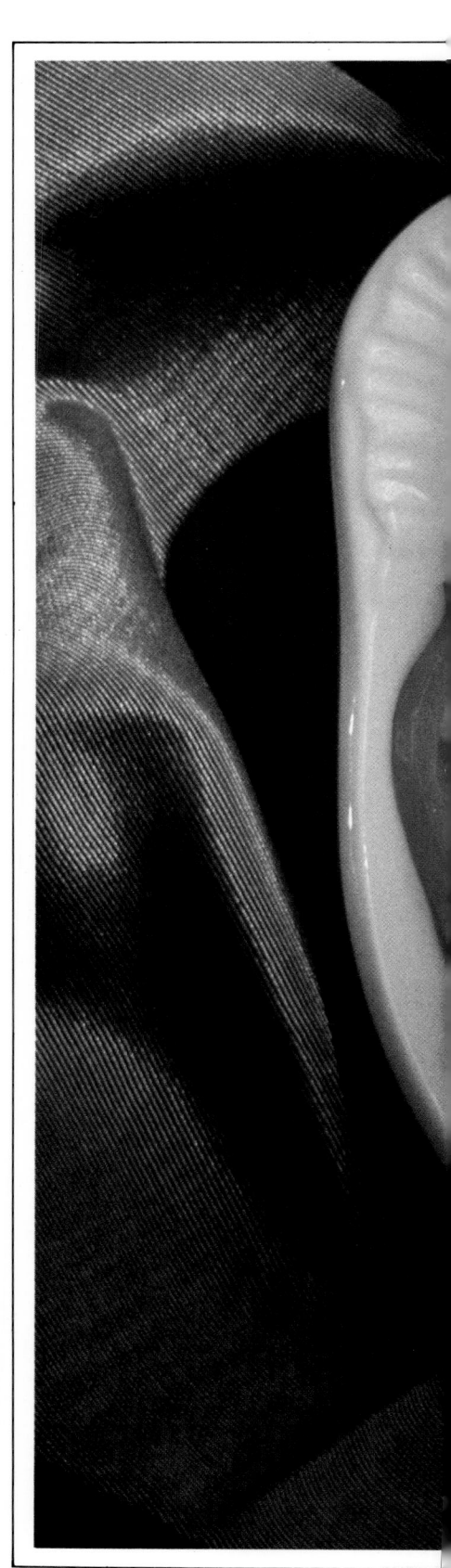

Macaroni with tuna fish

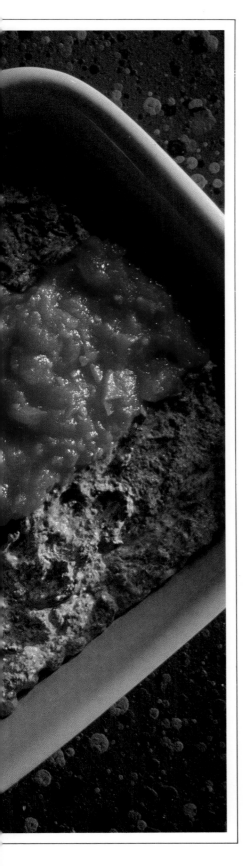

LASAGNE WITH SPINACH

SERVES 4 / SET: FULL AND MEDIUM

Ingredients
10–12 sheets lasagne
boiling water
salt
4 cups/1 kg/2 lb fresh spinach
³/4 cup/200 ml/¹/3 pt cream
250 g/8 oz ricotta cheese
freshly ground black pepper
nutmeg
15 ml/1 tbsp oil
1 clove garlic, crushed (minced)
1 small onion, finely chopped
³/4 cup/200 g/7 oz tinned (canned) tomatoes, sieved (strained)

◆ Put the lasagne sheets in a deep oblong dish and cover with boiling water. Add a pinch of salt and a few drops of oil, cover and cook on full power for 10 minutes. Allow to stand, covered, while you make the sauces.

◆ Wash the spinach and discard any tough stalks and discoloured leaves. Put it in a boiling or roasting bag, with only the water clinging to it, tie loosely and cook on full power for 6 minutes. Drain and chop roughly.

◆ Mix together the cream and ricotta cheese until well blended. Stir in the spinach and season with salt, pepper and nutmeg to taste.

◆ Assemble the lasagne in an oiled oblong dish. Layer the pasta and the spinach sauce until all are used up. Begin with a layer of pasta and end with a layer of sauce.

◆ Make the tomato sauce. Put the oil in a bowl, add the onion and garlic and cook on full power for 2 minutes. Add the sieved tomatoes and cook on full power for 2 minutes. Season to taste.

◆ Pour the tomato sauce over the lasagne and heat through on medium power for 4–5 minutes.

◆ Serve hot.

Lasagne with spinach

PAPPARDELLE WITH CHICKEN LIVERS

SERVES 4 / SET: FULL

Ingredients
3¹/2 cups/400 g/14 oz pappardelle
boiling water
salt
a few drops of oil
15 ml/1 tbsp olive oil
30 ml/2 tbsp marsala
2 shallots, finely chopped
1 clove garlic, finely chopped
1 cup/250 g/8 oz chicken livers, trimmed and chopped
chopped parsley
lemon wedges

◆ Put the pappardelle in a deep pot and pour over enough boiling water to cover. Add a pinch of salt and a few drops of oil, cover and cook for 9 minutes. Leave to stand, covered, while you prepare the sauce.

◆ Put the oil and marsala in a dish with the shallots and garlic. Cover and cook for 2 minutes. Stir in the chicken livers, and cook for 2–3 minutes, stirring once, until just done.

◆ Drain the pasta and top with the sauce. Sprinkle with chopped parsley and serve with lemon wedges.

TAGLIATELLE WITH ASPARAGUS SPEARS

SERVES 4 / SET: FULL

Ingredients

400 g/14 oz tagliatelle
boiling water
salt
oil
²/₃ cup/150 ml/¹/₄ pt single (light) cream
3¹/₂ cups/400 g/14 oz freshly cooked or tinned (canned) asparagus spears
Parmesan cheese

◆ Put the tagliatelle in a deep pot and just cover with boiling water. Add a pinch of salt and a few drops of oil, cover and cook for 6 minutes. Set aside, covered.

◆ Put the cream in a bowl and stir in the asparagus spears. Cook for 2 minutes.

◆ Drain the pasta, pour over the sauce and serve with plenty of Parmesan cheese.

Tagliatelle with asparagus

LINGUINE WITH BACON AND CHICKEN

SERVES 4 / SET: FULL

Ingredients.

400 g/14 oz linguine

boiling water

salt

a few drops of oil

3 tbsp/40 g/1½ oz butter

1 shallot, chopped

2 large tomatoes, peeled, seeded and chopped

¾ cup/125 g/5 oz cooked chicken, chopped

2 rashers (strips) bacon, cooked and chopped

freshly ground black pepper

◆ Put the linguine in a dish and pour over enough boiling water to cover. Add a pinch of salt and a few drops of oil, cover and cook for 9 minutes. Leave to stand, covered, while you prepare the sauce.

◆ Put the butter in a dish and cook for 45 seconds. Add the shallot and cook for 2 minutes. Add the tomatoes, chicken and bacon and cook for 3 minutes, stirring once, until hot. Season to taste.

◆ Drain the linguine, top with the sauce and serve at once.

HAY AND STRAW

SERVES 4 / SET: FULL

Ingredients

200 g/7 oz yellow tagliatelle
200 g/7 oz green tagliatelle
boiling water
salt
oil
²⁄₃ cup/100 g/4 oz Parma ham, chopped
²⁄₃ cup/150 ml/¼ pt single (light) cream
freshly ground black pepper
Parmesan cheese

The Italian name of this dish is paglia e
fieno. *'Hay and straw' refers to the two
colours of tagliatelle used. It is very quick
to make.*

◆ Put the yellow and green
tagliatelle together in a deep pot and
pour on enough boiling water to just
cover. Add a pinch of salt and a few
drops of oil. Cover and cook for
6 minutes. Let the pot stand, covered,
while you make the sauce.
◆ Stir the ham and cream together
in a bowl and season with black
pepper. Cook for 2 minutes.
◆ Drain the pasta, stir in the sauce
and serve with plenty of Parmesan
cheese.

Hay and straw

SPAGHETTI WITH FETA CHEESE AND BLACK OLIVES

SERVES 4 / SET: FULL

Ingredients

400 g/14 oz spaghetti

4½ cups/1 l/1¾ pt boiling water

salt

45 ml/3 tbsp olive oil

1 clove garlic, crushed (minced)

12 black olives, stoned (pitted) and chopped

1¼ cups/125 g/5 oz feta cheese, crumbled

4 sage leaves, chopped

freshly ground black pepper

◆ Hold the spaghetti in a pot and pour on the boiling water. Push the spaghetti down into the water and add a pinch of salt and a few drops of oil. Cover and cook for 12 minutes. Leave the pot to stand, covered, while you make the sauce.

◆ Put the oil in a dish and cook for 45 seconds. Add the garlic and cook for 1 minute. Add the olives and cook for 30 seconds.

◆ Add the feta cheese to the hot oil, with the chopped sage. Grind on a little black pepper and mix the sauce well.

◆ Drain the spaghetti and stir in the sauce.

◆ Serve at once.

PASTA BOWS WITH CHICKEN LIVERS

SERVES 4 / SET: FULL

Ingredients
3½ cups/400 g/14 oz farfalle (pasta bows)
boiling water
salt
oil
1 cup/250 g/8 oz chicken livers, chopped
30 ml/2 tbsp marsala
1 clove garlic, crushed (minced)
cayenne pepper
Parmesan cheese

◆ Put the pasta into a deep pot and just cover with boiling water. Add a pinch of salt and a few drops of oil and cook, covered, for 9 minutes. Let the pot stand, covered, while you make the sauce.
◆ Put the chicken livers, marsala and garlic in a bowl and cook, covered, for 3 minutes.
◆ Drain the pasta, pour on the sauce, sprinkle with cayenne pepper and serve with Parmesan cheese.

PASTA

TAGLIATELLE WITH ANCHOVIES AND TUNA FISH

SERVES 4 / SET: FULL

Ingredients

30 ml/2 tbsp olive oil
1 clove garlic, crushed (minced)
4 anchovy fillets, drained, soaked in milk, rinsed and chopped
½ cup/100 g/4 oz tinned (canned) tuna fish, drained
30 ml/2 tbsp capers
50 g/2 oz black olives, stoned (pitted)
400 g/14 oz tagliatelle
boiling water
salt
chopped parsley

◆ Put the oil in a bowl and add the garlic. Cook for 1 minute. Stir in the anchovies, tuna, capers and olives, cover and cook for 3 minutes.

◆ Put the tagliatelle in a deep pot and just cover with boiling water. Add a pinch of salt and a few drops of oil, cover and cook for 6 minutes. Let the pot stand for 3 minutes and reheat the sauce for 2 minutes while it is waiting.

◆ Drain the pasta, pour over the sauce and garnish with chopped parsley.

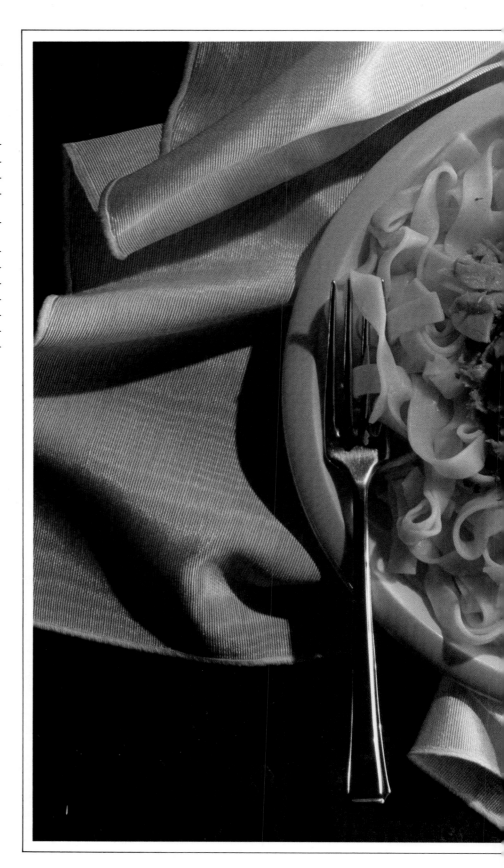

Tagliatelle with anchovies and tuna

LASAGNE WITH LEEKS AND SAUSAGE

SERVES 4 / SET: FULL

Ingredients

2 large leeks, sliced

1 1/3 cups/250 g/8 oz spicy sausage, sliced

3/4 cup/200 g/7 oz sieved (strained) tomatoes (passata)

a pinch dried mixed herbs

6 sheets spinach lasagne

boiling water

a few drops of oil

3 tbsp/40 g/1 1/2 oz butter

6 tbsp/40 g/1 1/2 oz flour

1 1/4 cups/300 ml/1/2 pt milk

1/2 cup/50 g/2 oz grated cheese

freshly ground black pepper / salt

60 ml/4 tbsp breadcrumbs

◆ Put the leeks and sausage in a deep oblong dish with 60 ml/4 tbsp of the strained sieved tomatoes. Cover with vented cling wrap (plastic wrap) and cook for 6 minutes, stirring once. Add the rest of the sieved tomato and the herbs, season, and set aside.

◆ Put the lasagne in a deep pot and pour over enough boiling water to cover. Add a pinch of salt and a few drops of oil, cover and cook for 15 minutes. Drain and rinse thoroughly under cold running water. Lay the pasta on a tea towel to dry. (Do not use kitchen paper.)

◆ Make the cheese sauce. Put the butter in a dish and cook for 1 minute. Stir in the flour. Pour on the milk. Cook for 3 minutes, whisking after each minute. Stir in the cheese. Cook for a further minute and whisk again. Season to taste.

◆ Assemble the dish in layers until all the ingredients are used up, finishing with a layer of cheese sauce.

◆ Top with breadcrumbs and heat through in the microwave or, if you would like the dish to brown, in a conventional oven or grill (broiler).

◆ Serve hot.

CHICKEN LASAGNE

SERVES 4 / SET: FULL AND MEDIUM

Ingredients

10–12 sheets lasagne
boiling water
salt
oil
3 tbsp/40 g/1½ oz butter
1 onion, chopped
1 clove garlic, chopped
2 cups/100 g/4 oz mushrooms, sliced
5 ml/1 tsp dried oregano
6 tbsp/40 g/1½ oz flour
2 cups/450 ml/¾ pt milk
1 chicken stock (bouillon) cube
1⅔ cups/300 g/10 oz cooked chicken, chopped
4½ tbsp/40 g/1½ oz grated Parmesan cheese, plus extra for the topping

◆ Put the lasagne sheets in a deep oblong dish and cover with boiling water. Add a pinch of salt and a few drops of oil, cover and cook on full power for 10 minutes. Allow to stand, covered, while you make the sauce.

◆ Put the butter in a bowl and cook on full power for 1 minute. Stir in the onion and garlic and cook on full power for 2 minutes. Stir in the mushrooms and oregano and cook on full power for 2 minutes.

◆ Stir in the flour and gradually add the milk, stirring. Crumble on the stock (bouillon) cube. Cook on full power for 3 minutes, stirring after each minute. Stir in the chicken and cheese and cook on full power for 1 minute. Keep warm.

◆ Drain the lasagne and lay the sheets out on a tea towel.

◆ Assemble. In an oiled oblong dish, layer the pasta and sauce until both are used up. Start with a layer of pasta and end with a layer of sauce. Sprinkle more Parmesan cheese on the top and cook on medium power for 5 minutes, turning the dish once.

◆ Serve hot.

TAGLIATELLE WITH MUSSELS AND PRAWNS (SHRIMP)

SERVES 4 / SET: FULL

Ingredients

15 ml/1 tbsp olive oil

1 clove garlic, crushed (minced)

¾ cup/200 g/7 oz tinned (canned) tomatoes, drained and mashed

2½ ml/½ tsp dried basil, or fresh basil to taste, snipped

freshly ground black pepper

250 g/8 oz peeled prawns (shrimp), plus a few unpeeled ones for garnish

400 g/14 oz tagliatelle

boiling water

salt

5 cups/600 ml/1 pt mussels, scrubbed clean

1 glass dry white wine

chopped parsley

◆ Put the oil in a bowl and cook for 30 seconds. Add the garlic and cook for 1 minute. Add the tomatoes, basil, pepper and peeled prawns (shrimp) and cook for 4 minutes. Season with salt to taste, set aside and keep warm.

◆ Put the tagliatelle in a deep pot and pour over enough boiling water to just cover. Add a pinch of salt and a few drops of oil, cover and cook for 6 minutes. Set aside, covered.

◆ Discard any broken or open mussels and put the rest in a deep pot. Pour over the white wine. Add parsley to taste. Cover and cook for 3 minutes, or until the mussels open.

◆ Remove some mussels from their shells and stir into the sauce. Drain the pasta, pour over the sauce and garnish with the remaining mussels and the unpeeled prawns.

TAGLIATELLE BOLOGNESE

SERVES 4 / SET: FULL

Ingredients
15 ml/1 tbsp oil
1 clove garlic, crushed (minced)
1 onion, finely chopped
1 carrot, finely chopped
1 stick (stack) celery, finely chopped
3/4 cup/200 g/7 oz tinned (canned) tomatoes, drained and mashed
1 scant cup/200 g/7 oz minced (ground) beef
1/3 cup/50 g/2 oz ham
30 ml/2 tbsp red wine
1 bayleaf
3 chicken livers, chopped
salt and freshly ground black pepper
400 g/14 oz tagliatelle
boiling water
Parmesan cheese

◆ Put the oil in a bowl and cook for 30 seconds. Add the garlic, onion, carrot and celery and cook for 2 minutes. Stir in the tomatoes, beef and ham and add the red win to moisten. Tuck the bayleaf into the mixture. Cook for 5 minutes, stirring once.
◆ Add the chicken livers and cook for 2 minutes. Season, set aside and keep warm.
◆ Put the tagliatelle in a deep pot and pour over enough boiling water to just cover. Add a pinch of salt and a few drops of oil, cover and cook for 6 minutes. Leave to stand, covered, for 3 minutes while you reheat the sauce if necessary.
◆ Drain the pasta, pour over the sauce and serve with plenty of Parmesan cheese.

Tagliatelle bolognese

BUCATINI WITH RED LENTIL SAUCE

SERVES 4 / SET: FULL

Ingredients
15 ml/1 tbsp oil
1 onion, chopped
1 clove garlic, chopped
3/4 cup/200 g/7 oz tinned (canned) tomatoes, drained and mashed
salt and freshly ground black pepper
scant cup/125 g/5 oz red lentils
1 1/4 cups/300 ml/1/2 pt boiling water
3 1/2 cups/400 g/14 oz bucatini
Parmesan cheese

◆ Put the oil in a dish and cook for 30 seconds. Add the onion and garlic, cover and cook for 2 minutes. Add the tomatoes and seasoning. Set aside.
◆ Put the lentils in a pot and pour over the boiling water. Cover and cook for 12 minutes. Stir in the tomato sauce and set aside.
◆ Put the bucatini in a deep pot. Cover with boiling water and add a few drops of oil. Cover and cook for 9 minutes. Set aside.
◆ Reheat the sauce.
◆ Drain the bucatini, stir in the sauce and serve topped with plenty of Parmesan cheese.

STUFFED CANNELLONI

S E R V E S   4 / S E T :   F U L L

Ingredients

15 ml/1 tbsp oil
1 onion, finely chopped
1 carrot, finely chopped
1 stick (stack) celery, finely chopped
30 ml/2 tbsp red wine
15 ml/1 tbsp tomato purée (paste)
1 scant cup/200 g/7 oz lean minced (ground) beef
1 scant cup/200 g/7 oz lean minced (ground) veal
²/₃ cup/100 g/4 oz ham, chopped
250 g/8 oz cannelloni
boiling water
3 tbsp/40 g/1¹/₂ oz butter
6 tbsp/40 g/1¹/₂ oz flour
1¹/₄ cups/300 ml/¹/₂ pt milk
freshly ground black pepper
nutmeg
4¹/₂ tbsp/40 g/1¹/₂ oz Parmesan cheese, grated
1 egg yolk

◆ First make the stuffing. Put the oil in a bowl and cook for 30 seconds. Stir in the onion, carrot and celery and cook for 2 minutes. Stir in the wine mixed with the tomato purée (paste). Add the beef, veal and ham and combine well. Cover and cook for 5 minutes, until done. Season with salt and pepper.

◆ Put the cannelloni in a deep oblong dish and just cover with boiling water. Add a pinch of salt and a few drops of oil. Cover and cook for 9 minutes. Leave for 3 minutes, covered, then drain and stuff with the meat mixture.

◆ Meanwhile, make the sauce. Put the butter in a bowl and cook for 1 minute. Stir in the flour and cook for 1 minute. Pour on the milk and cook for 3 minutes, whisking after every minute. Add salt and pepper and a little nutmeg to taste. Stir in the Parmesan cheese and cook for a further minute. Whisk again, then stir in the egg yolk.

◆ Lay the stuffed cannelloni in a greased dish, in a single layer if possible. Pour over the sauce. Cover with vented cling wrap (plastic wrap) and cook for 1–2 minutes to heat through.

◆ Serve hot.

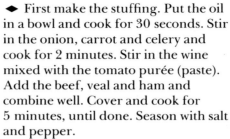

LINGUINE WITH MUSHROOM SAUCE

SERVES 4 / SET: FULL

Ingredients

2¹/₂ cups/250 g/8 oz mushrooms, wiped and sliced

30 ml/2 tbsp milk

400 g/14 oz green linguine

boiling water

salt

oil

²/₃ cup/150 ml/5 fl oz single (light) cream

chopped parsley

◆ Put the mushrooms in a dish and add the milk. Cover and cook for 3 minutes, stirring once. Set aside.

◆ Put the linguine in a deep pot and pour over enough boiling water to cover. Add a pinch of salt and a few drops of oil. Cover and cook for 9 minutes. Set aside.

◆ Stir the cream into the mushrooms. Reheat for 1 minute.

◆ Drain the pasta, pour on the mushrooms, garnish with parsley and serve.

TAGLIATELLE WITH PEAS AND CREAM

SERVES 4 / SET: FULL

Ingredients

400 g/14 oz tagliatelle

boiling water

salt

oil

²/₃ cup/150 ml/¹/₄ pt double (heavy) cream

3¹/₂ cups/400 g/14 oz cooked peas (or use canned peas)

¹/₂ cup/50 g/2 oz Emmenthal cheese, grated

¹/₃ cup/50 g/2 oz Parmesan cheese, grated

strips of pepper

◆ Put the tagliatelle in a pot and pour over enough boiling water to just cover. Add a pinch of salt and a few drops of oil, cover and cook for 6 minutes. Leave to stand, covered.

◆ Pour the cream into a bowl and stir in the peas. Cook for 1¹/₂ minutes. Stir in both cheeses and cook for 1¹/₂ minutes, stirring twice, until melted.

◆ Drain the tagliatelle, stir in the sauce and serve at once garnished with strips of pepper.

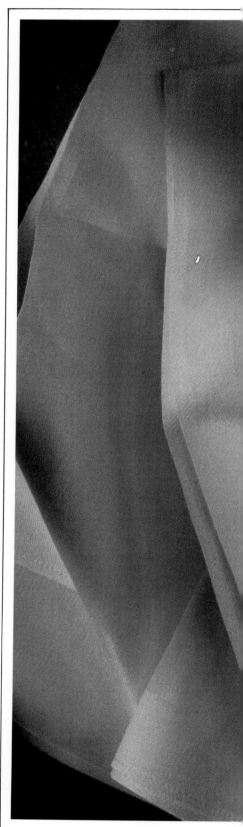

Tagliatelle with peas and cream

LINGUINE WITH GREEN BEANS, TOMATOES AND PUMPKIN SEEDS

SERVES 4 / SET: FULL

Ingredients

2 cups/250 g/8 oz green beans, topped and tailed (trimmed) and cut into bite size pieces
30 ml/2 tbsp water
¾ cup/250 g/8 oz tomatoes, peeled, seeded and cut into strips
50 g/2 oz pumpkin seeds
400 g/14 oz green linguine
boiling water
salt
15–30 ml/1–2 tbsp oil
Parmesan cheese (optional)

◆ Put the beans in a dish with the water, cover with vented cling wrap (plastic wrap) and cook for 4 minutes.

◆ Add the tomatoes and cook for a further 4 minutes. Add the pumpkin seeds. Keep covered and keep warm.

◆ Put the linguine in a deep pot with enough boiling water to cover. Add a pinch of salt and a few drops of oil. Cover and cook for 8 minutes. Set aside, covered.

◆ Drain the vegetables and dress with the oil. Reheat, covered, for 1 minute.

◆ Drain the pasta and mix in the vegetables.

◆ Serve with Parmesan cheese if liked.

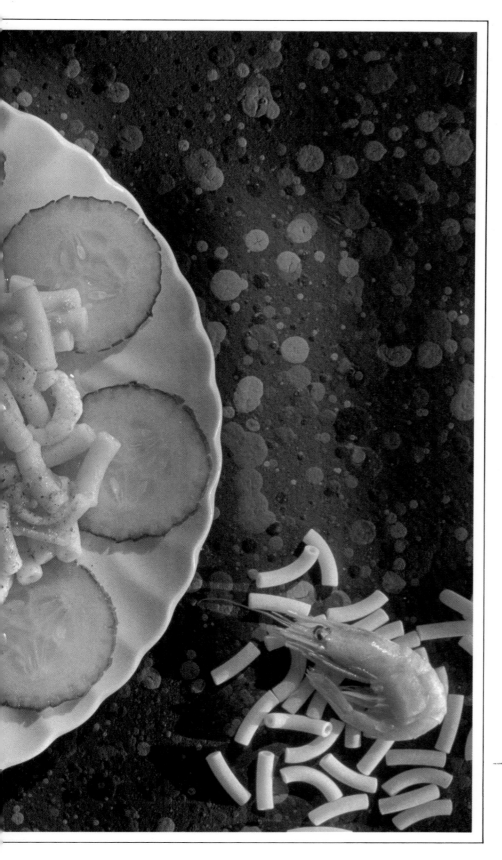

MACARONI WITH PRAWNS (SHRIMP)

S E R V E S   4   /   S E T :   F U L L

Ingredients

15 ml/1 tbsp oil
2 cloves garlic, crushed (minced)
1 red chilli (chili), seeded and chopped
400 g/14 oz tinned (canned) tomatoes, drained and mashed
1½ cups/350 g/12 oz shelled prawns (shrimp)
15 ml/1 tbsp lemon juice
freshly ground black pepper
a sprig of thyme
1 bayleaf
a few sprigs of parsley
3½ cups/400 g/14 oz macaroni
boiling water
salt
cucumber slices

◆ Put the oil in a bowl and cook for 30 seconds. Add the garlic and chilli (chili) and cook for 1 minute. Stir in the tomatoes and cook for 3 minutes. Stir in the prawns (shrimp) and lemon juice, sprinkle with black pepper and add the herbs. Cover and cook for 2 minutes.

◆ Put the macaroni in a bowl and just cover with boiling water. Add a pinch of salt and a few drops of oil, cover and cook for 10 minutes. Leave to stand for 3 minutes. Reheat the sauce if necessary.

◆ Drain the pasta and mix in the sauce.

◆ Garnish with cucumber slices and serve hot.

Macaroni with prawns (shrimp)

PASTA

BUCATINI ALL'AMATRICIANA

S E R V E S   4 / S E T :   F U L L

Ingredients

¹/₂ cup/75 g/3 oz bacon, derinded (trimmed) and chopped

2 tbsp/25 g/1 oz butter

1 onion, finely chopped

1¹/₂ cups/400 g/14 oz tinned (canned) tomatoes, drained and mashed

1³/₄ cups/200 g/7 oz tinned (canned) peas, drained

salt

3¹/₂ cups/400 g/14 oz bucatini

boiling water

salt

oil

grated pecorino cheese

◆ Put the bacon on a plate covered with absorbent kitchen paper. Cook for 2 minutes. Set aside.

◆ Put the butter in a bowl and cook for 1 minute. Add the onion and cook for 2 minutes. Stir in the tomatoes and cook for 2 minutes. Stir in the peas and bacon and cook for 2 minutes.

◆ Put the bucatini in a pot and just cover with boiling water. Add a pinch of salt and a few drops of oil, cover and cook for 10 minutes. Set aside, covered. Reheat the sauce if necessary during standing time.

◆ Drain the pasta, top with the sauce and serve with grated pecorino cheese.

SPAGHETTI WITH MANGETOUT (SNOW) PEAS

SERVES 4 / SET: FULL

Ingredients

15 ml/1 tbsp oil
25 g/1 oz butter
1 clove garlic, crushed (minced)
¾ cup/100 g/4 oz mangetout (snow) peas, stalks removed
1¼ cups/100 g/4 oz button mushrooms, wiped and sliced
scant ½ cup/100 g/4 oz fresh tomatoes, skinned and chopped
salt, freshly ground black pepper
400 g/14 oz spaghetti
4½ cups/1 l/1¾ pt boiling water
chopped fresh herbs
Parmesan cheese

◆ Put the oil in a bowl with the butter and cook for 1 minute. Add the garlic and cook for 1 minute. Stir in the mangetout peas, mushrooms and tomatoes. Cover with vented cling wrap (plastic wrap) and cook for 3 minutes. Season and set aside.

◆ Hold the spaghetti in a deep pot. Pour over the boiling water and push the spaghetti down into the pot. Add a pinch of salt and a few drops of oil, cover and cook for 12 minutes. Leave to stand, covered, for 5 minutes. Reheat the sauce during standing time if necessary.

◆ Drain the pasta and top with the sauce. Sprinkle with fresh herbs and offer Parmesan cheese at the table.

FARFALLE AL GORGONZOLA

SERVES 4 / SET: FULL

Ingredients

175–250 g/6–8 oz ripe gorgonzola cheese

2/3 cup/150 ml/1/4 pt double (heavy) or single (light) cream

3 1/2 cups/400 g/14 oz farfalle (bow-shaped) pasta

boiling water

salt

oil

freshly ground black pepper

This is a luxurious dish that can be prepared very quickly.

◆ If necessary, soften the cheese by putting it, wrapped, in the microwave for a few seconds on defrost power. Cream the cheese with the cream in the liquidizer. Put the mixture in a bowl and cook for 2 minutes to warm through.

◆ Put the pasta in a deep pot and just cover with boiling water. Add a pinch of salt and a few drops of oil, cover and cook for 10 minutes. Leave to stand for 3 minutes.

◆ Heat the sauce through again if necessary during the standing time. It should be warm, not hot.

◆ Drain the pasta and stir in the sauce. Offer black pepper at the table.

Farfalle al gorgonzola

BEAN-STUFFED CANNELLONI

SERVES 4 / SET: FULL

Ingredients

2 cups/400 g/14 oz tinned (canned) cannellini beans, drained

2/3 cup/100 g/4 oz ricotta cheese

1 bunch parsley, chopped

1 onion, chopped

3/4 cup/250 g/8 oz tomatoes, skinned, peeled and chopped

salt and freshly ground black pepper

8 cannelloni

boiling water

a few drops of oil

2/3 cup/150 ml/1/4 pt single (light) cream

When cooked like this, the onion and tomato in the stuffing will still be crisp and firm respectively, which makes a refreshing change.

◆ Make the stuffing by mixing together the beans, ricotta, parsley, onion and tomatoes, and season well with salt and pepper.

◆ Put the cannelloni in a deep oblong dish and cover with boiling water. Add a few drops of oil and a pinch of salt. Cover and cook for 12 minutes. Drain and rinse under cold running water.

◆ Stuff the cannelloni with the bean mixture and arrange in the dish. Pour the cream over and reheat for 2 minutes.

◆ Serve at once.

GREEN TAGLIATELLE WITH PEPPERS

S E R V E S   4 / S E T :   F U L L

Ingredients

15 ml/1 tbsp olive oil
1 small onion, chopped
1 clove garlic, crushed (minced)
1½ cups/400 g/14 oz tinned (canned) tomatoes, drained
salt and freshly ground black pepper
½ red pepper, cut into strips about 2.5 cm/ 1 in long
½ green pepper, cut into strips about 2.5 cm/1 in long
½ yellow pepper, cut into strips about 2.5 cm/1 in long
30 ml/2 tbsp water
400 g/14 oz spinach tagliatelle
boiling water
salt
Parmesan cheese

◆ Put the oil in a bowl and cook for 30 seconds. Add the onion and garlic and cook for 2 minutes. Add the tomatoes and cook for 2 minutes. Purée in a liquidizer and season to taste.

◆ Put the pepper strips in a bowl and add the water. Cover with vented cling wrap (plastic wrap) and cook for 4 minutes, until tender. Set aside.

◆ Put the tagliatelle in a deep pot and just cover with boiling water. Add a pinch of salt and a few drops of oil, cover and cook for 6 minutes. Leave to stand for 3 minutes. Reheat the sauce if necessary during standing time.

◆ Drain the pasta, pour over the sauce and garnish with the strips of pepper.

◆ Serve with Parmesan cheese.

TAGLIATELLE WITH SPINACH AND WALNUT SAUCE

SERVES 4 / SET: FULL

Ingredients

2 cups/500 g/1 lb fresh spinach

4 rashers (strips) bacon, derinded (trimmed) and chopped

15 g/½ oz butter

1 clove garlic, crushed (minced)

⅔ cup/150 ml/5 fl oz single (light) cream

⅓ cup/50 g/2 oz walnut pieces

400 g/14 oz tagliatelle

boiling water

salt

oil

Parmesan cheese

◆ Wash the spinach and discard any tough leaves and stalks. Put it into a roasting or boiling bag with only the water clinging to it, tie loosely and cook for 6 minutes, until the leaves have collapsed. Purée the spinach in a blender.

◆ Put the bacon on a plate covered with absorbent kitchen paper and cook for 2 minutes until done.

◆ Put the butter in a small bowl with the garlic, add the bacon and cook for 2 minutes.

◆ Stir the spinach into the cream, add the walnuts and cook for 4 minutes. Set aside, covered.

◆ Put the tagliatelle in a deep bowl and just cover with boiling water. Add a pinch of salt and a few drops of oil and cook for 6 minutes. Let the bowl stand, covered, while you reheat the spinach cream sauce if necessary.

◆ Drain the pasta and stir in the cream sauce. Top with the garlic and bacon.

◆ Serve hot with Parmesan cheese.

LASAGNE WITH FISH

SERVES 4 / SET: FULL

Ingredients

6 sheets lasagne

boiling water

salt

oil

1 cup/250 g/8 oz cooked white fish, flaked

generous cup/200 g/7 oz tinned (canned) sweetcorn (corn), drained

3/4 cup/200 g/7 oz sieved (strained) tomatoes (passata)

chopped parsley

freshly ground black pepper

3 tbsp/40 g/1 1/2 oz butter

6 tbsp/40 g/1 1/2 oz flour

1 1/4 cups/300 ml/1/2 pt milk

1/2 cup/50 g/2 oz Edam cheese, grated

30 ml/2 tbsp Parmesan cheese

◆ Put the lasagne in a dish and pour over enough boiling water to cover. Add a pinch of salt and a few drops of oil. Cover and cook for 15 minutes. Drain and rinse well under cold running water. Lay the sheets on a tea towel to dry. (Do not use kitchen paper – it will stick.)

◆ Mix the fish, sweetcorn (corn), tomatoes and parsley together and season with salt and pepper.

◆ Put the butter in a bowl and cook for 1 minute. Stir in the flour. Pour on the milk and cook for 3 minutes, whisking after each minute. Stir in the Edam cheese and cook for a further minute. Whisk again. Season with salt and pepper.

◆ Assemble. Begin with a layer of fish and tomato, then cover with lasagne and top with cheese sauce. Continue until all the ingredients have been used up, ending with the cheese sauce. Sprinkle with Parmesan cheese.

◆ Heat through in the microwave, or under the grill (broiler) or in a conventional oven if you want the top to brown.

PENNE AL PESTO

SERVES 4 / SET: FULL

Ingredients

1 large bunch fresh basil

15 ml/1 tbsp pine nuts

4 cloves garlic

30 ml/2 tbsp grated Parmesan cheese

virgin olive oil

salt and freshly ground black pepper

3 1/2 cups/400 g/14 oz penne (pasta quills)

boiling water

This dish is a speciality of Genoa, on the Ligurian coast of Italy. Pesto sauce can be served equally well with rice.

◆ To make the pesto sauce snip the basil leaves into a mortar. Add the pine nuts and garlic and crush with the pestle. Add Parmesan cheese and olive oil, pounding all the while, until you have a thick paste. Season with salt and pepper. You can make the sauce by combining all the ingredients in a blender, but it is more satisfying by hand.

◆ Put the penne in a large pot and just cover with boiling water. Add a pinch of salt and a few drops of oil, cover and cook for 10 minutes. Leave to stand for a couple of minutes, then drain and stir in the sauce.

◆ Serve hot.

Penne al pesto

RIGATONI COUNTRY-STYLE

S E R V E S   4   /   S E T :   F U L L

Ingredients

3¹/₂ cups/400 g/14 oz rigatoni (or macaroni
boiling water
salt
oil
1 cup/175 g/6 oz spicy sausage, cut into chunks or sliced
1¹/₂ cups/100 g/4 oz cauliflower florets
15 ml/1 tbsp water
1 cup/100 g/4 oz green beans, topped and tailed (trimmed) and cut into bite size pieces
15–30 ml/1–2 tbsp olive oil
cayenne pepper
1 whole mozzarella cheese, diced

Use the long spicy sausages sold in coils for this dish. If you can't find these, use diced salami.

◆ Put the rigatoni in a deep pot and just cover with boiling water. Add a pinch of salt and a few drops of oil. Cover and cook for 10 minutes. Leave to stand, covered, while you make the sauce.

◆ Put the sausage pieces on a plate covered with absorbent kitchen paper and cook for 1¹/₂ minutes. Cover and keep warm.

◆ Put the cauliflower in a bowl with the water. Cover and cook for 1 minute. Add the beans, cover and cook for 3 minutes.

◆ Drain the pasta and vegetables. Pour the olive oil over the pasta and season with cayenne pepper. Stir in the cauliflower, beans, sausage and diced mozzarella cheese, cover and heat through for 1 minute.

◆ Serve hot.

Rigatoni countrystyle

LASAGNE AND HAM ROLLS

S E R V E S   4   /   S E T :   F U L L

Ingredients

4 sheets spinach lasagne
boiling water
salt
oil
4 slices ham, the same size as the lasagne sheets

This makes a tasty and attractive appetizer and it is also an unusual accompaniment to drinks. It is simple to prepare, but looks elegant.

◆ Put the lasagne in a deep pot with enough boiling water to cover. Add a pinch of salt and a few drops of oil. Cover and cook for 10 minutes. Leave to stand for 3 minutes. Drain and rinse well under cold running water.

◆ Lay the lasagne sheets out on a tea towel to dry. Do not use kitchen paper – it will stick to the pasta.

◆ When the lasagne has cooled, lay a slice of ham on top of each sheet and roll up tightly.

◆ Cut each roll into slices and serve cold.

SPAGHETTI WITH CLAMS

SERVES 4 / SET: FULL

Ingredients

6 cups/750 g/1½ lb clams
30 ml/2 tbsp olive oil
1 clove garlic, crushed (minced)
1½ cups/500 g/1 lb ripe tomatoes, peeled and chopped
salt and freshly ground black pepper
400 g/14 oz spaghetti
4½ cups/1 l/1¾ pt boiling water
a small glass of dry white wine
chopped parsley

This dish is one of the specialities of Naples.

◆ Clean the clams thoroughly under running water.

◆ Put the olive oil in a bowl and cook for 30 seconds. Add the garlic and cook for 1 minute. Add the tomatoes, cover with vented cling wrap (plastic wrap) and cook for 4 minutes, until soft. Season with salt and pepper and keep warm.

◆ Hold the spaghetti in a large pot and pour over it the boiling water. Push the spaghetti down into the water, add a pinch of salt and a few drops of oil, cover and cook for 2 minutes. Set aside, covered.

◆ Put the clams in a pot with the white wine, cover and cook for 2–3 minutes, until the shells open. Set aside.

◆ Drain the spaghetti and stir in the tomato sauce. Drain the clams and pile on top of the pasta.

◆ Sprinkle with parsley and serve hot.

VARIATION The clams may be removed from their shells before serving if you prefer.

Spaghetti with clams

MACARONI WITH BROCCOLI AND ALMONDS

SERVES 4 / SET: FULL

Ingredients

3 ½ cups/400 g/14 oz macaroni

boiling water

oil

salt

50 g/2 oz butter

generous 3 cups/250 g/8 oz broccoli florets

⅓ cup/50 g/2 oz flaked (slivered) toasted almonds

60 ml/4 tbsp grated pecorino cheese

◆ Put the macaroni in a deep pot and pour over enough boiling water to cover. Add a few drops of oil and a pinch of salt, cover and cook for 9 minutes. allow to stand.

◆ Put half the butter in a dish and cook for 1 minute. Add the broccoli and almonds and cook for 6 minutes, stirring twice, until the broccoli is tender, but still crisp.

◆ Drain the pasta, add the rest of the butter and the broccoli and almonds, toss and sprinkle with grated cheese before serving.

PASTA

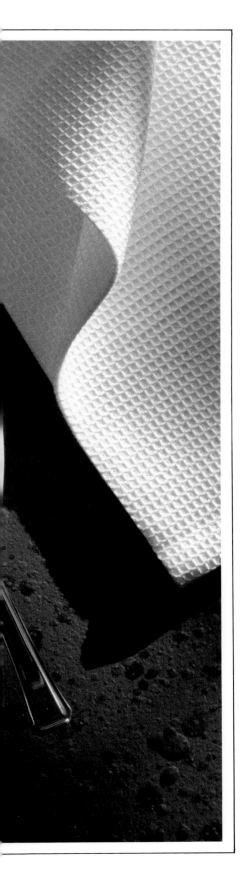

SPAGHETTI ALLA PUTANESCA

SERVES 4 / SET: FULL

Ingredients
400 g/14 oz spaghetti
4½ cups/1 l/1¾ pt boiling water
salt
oil
2 cloves garlic, chopped
½ cup/50 g/2 oz black olives, stoned (pitted) and roughly chopped
15 ml/1 tbsp capers, roughly chopped
5 anchovies, soaked in milk, rinsed, dried and chopped
1 red chilli (chili), seeded and chopped
30 ml/2 tbsp olive oil
¾ cup/200 g/7 oz tinned (canned) tomatoes, drained and chopped
chopped parsley

Legend has it that this dish was prepared by the whores of Rome. It is hot and fiery.

◆ Hold the spaghetti in a pot and pour the boiling water over it. Push the spaghetti down into the pot, add a pinch of salt and a few drops of oil, cover and cook for 12 minutes. Set aside, covered.
◆ Put the garlic, olives, capers, anchovies, chilli (chili) and olive oil in a bowl. Stir well, cover and cook for 2 minutes. Stir in the tomatoes, cover and cook for 3 minutes.
◆ Drain the spaghetti, stir in the sauce and top with chopped parsley to serve.

Spaghetti alla putanesca

PASTA AND FISH SALAD

SERVES 4 / SET: FULL

Ingredients
3½ cups/400 g/14 oz farfalle
boiling water
salt
30 ml/2 tbsp oil
scant cup/200 g/7 oz tinned (canned) tuna in brine, drained and flaked
2 pink onions, chopped
1 cup/200 g/7 oz tinned (canned) kidney beans, drained
freshly ground black pepper
chopped parsley
lemon wedges

◆ Put the farfalle in a pot and pour on enough boiling water to cover. Add a pinch of salt and a few drops of oil, cover and cook for 9 minutes. Drain and rinse thoroughly under cold running water. Drain thoroughly.
◆ Toss the pasta in the oil, add the tuna, onions and kidney beans and mix well.
◆ Season with salt and pepper, sprinkle with parsley and serve with lemon wedges.

PASTA AND HAM SALAD

SERVES 4 / SET: FULL

Ingredients

3½ cups/400 g/14 oz shell pasta
boiling water
salt
a few drops of oil
⅔ cup/100 g/4 oz diced ham
2 cups/200 g/7 oz cooked broad (java) beans (or use tinned (canned) beans, drained)
⅔ cup/150 ml/5 fl oz soured (sour) cream
freshly ground black pepper
mint leaves

◆ Put the pasta in a dish and pour over enough boiling water to cover. Add a pinch of salt and a few drops of oil, cover and cook for 9 minutes. Drain and rinse thoroughly under cold running water. Drain thoroughly.
◆ Toss the pasta with the ham and broad (java) beans in the soured (sour) cream. Season with salt and pepper and garnish with mint leaves.

PASTA WITH CHICK PEAS (GARBANZOS)

SERVES 4 / SET: FULL

Ingredients

3½ cups/400 g/14 oz multi-coloured pasta
boiling water
salt
15 ml/1 tbsp oil
2 tbsp/25 g/1 oz butter
1 clove garlic, crushed (minced)
2 cups/400 g/14 oz tinned (canned) chick peas (garbanzos), drained
⅓–½ cup/50–75 g/2–3 oz freshly grated Parmesan cheese
freshly ground black pepper

This is a very simple dish called "thunder and lightning" in Italy. Make it with canned chick peas (garbanzos) to save time.

◆ Put the pasta in a bowl and just cover with boiling water. Add a pinch of salt and a few drops of oil, cover and cook for 10 minutes. Allow to stand, covered.
◆ Put the butter in a bowl and cook for 1 minute. Stir in the garlic and chick peas (garbanzos), cover and cook for 2 minutes.
◆ Drain the pasta. Pour over the oil and the garlic chick peas and add the Parmesan cheese.
◆ Stir and serve at once. Offer black pepper at the table.

Pasta with chick peas (garbanzos)

SPAGHETTI WITH SQUID

S E R V E S   4   /   S E T :   F U L L

Ingredients

1³/4 cups/400 g/14 oz small squid
30 ml/2 tbsp olive oil
1 onion, finely chopped
1 clove garlic, crushed (minced)
1 stick (stack) celery, finely sliced
1 carrot, finely chopped
15 ml/1 tbsp lemon juice
chopped parsley
salt and freshly ground black pepper
400 g/14 oz spaghetti
4¹/2 cups/1 l/1³/4 pt boiling water (approx.)

◆ Remove the eyes and mouth of the squid, take out the cuttlefish bone and wash the squid thoroughly, peeling off the outer skin as you do so. Cut the body and tentacles into slices.

◆ Put the oil in a pot and cook for 30 seconds. Add the onion, garlic, celery, carrot and squid, sprinkle with lemon juice, cover and cook for 5 minutes. Stir in the parsley and season with salt and pepper.

◆ Hold the spaghetti in a pot and pour the water over it. As the spaghetti softens, push it down into the water. Add a pinch of salt and a few drops of oil, cover and cook for 12 minutes. Leave to stand for 5 minutes while you reheat the squid mixture.

◆ Drain the spaghetti and stir in the sauce. Serve at once.

Spaghetti with squid

SPINACH AND RICOTTA ROLLS

S E R V E S   4   /   S E T :   F U L L

Ingredients

4 cups/1 kg/2 lb fresh spinach

1¼ cups/250 g/8 oz ricotta cheese

salt and freshly ground black pepper

freshly grated nutmeg

8 sheets lasagne

boiling water

15 ml/1 tbsp oil

1 clove garlic, crushed (minced)

1 small onion, chopped

1½ cups/400 g/14 oz tinned (canned) tomatoes, sieved (strained)

◆ Wash the spinach and remove tough stalks and discoloured leaves. Put it in a roasting or boiling bag, tie loosely and cook for 6 minutes, shaking the bag once. Allow to cool.

◆ Chop the spinach, draining away excess moisture. Mix it well with the ricotta and season with salt, pepper and nutmeg.

◆ Put the lasagne in a dish and pour over enough boiling water to cover. Add a pinch of salt and a few drops of oil. Cover and cook for 15 minutes. Drain and rinse thoroughly under cold running water. Lay the lasagne sheets out on a tea towel to dry.

◆ Meanwhile, make the sauce. Put the oil in a bowl and cook for 30 seconds. Add the garlic and onion and cook for 3 minutes. Stir in the sieved (strained) tomato and cook for 4 minutes. Season to taste with salt and pepper.

◆ To assemble, divide the spinach and ricotta mixture between the lasagne sheets. Spread it out to cover the lasagne and roll each sheet up. Pack them in a dish they just fit and pour over the hot tomato sauce.

◆ Heat through in the microwave for a couple of minutes and serve hot.

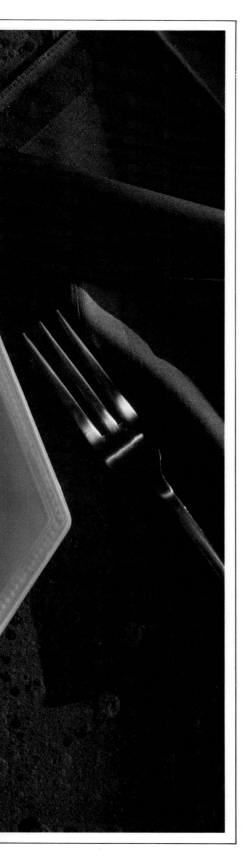

SPAGHETTI ALLA CARBONARA

SERVES 4 / SET: FULL AND MEDIUM

Ingredients
400 g/14 oz spaghetti
4½ cups/1 l/1¾ pt boiling water
salt
oil
⅔ cup/150 ml/5 fl oz double (heavy) cream
2 tbsp/25 g/1 oz butter
4 eggs
60 ml/4 tbsp grated Parmesan cheese
½ cup/75 g/3 oz diced ham (or gammon)
freshly ground black pepper

This favourite Roman dish is named after the charcoal burners who are said to have invented it.

◆ Put the spaghetti in a pot and pour on the boiling water. Push the spaghetti down into the pot. Add a pinch of salt and a few drops of oil. Cover the pot and cook on full for 12 minutes. Leave to stand, covered.
◆ Put the cream in a bowl with the butter and heat through on medium for 1½ minutes. Break in the eggs and beat well. Stir in the Parmesan and ham (or gammon) and season with black pepper. Cook on medium for 2–3 minutes, until the eggs are almost cooked and lightly scrambled in the cream, stirring twice.
◆ Drain the spaghetti, stir in the hot sauce and serve at once.

Spaghetti alla carbonara

SPAGHETTI MASCARPONE

SERVES 4 / SET: FULL

Ingredients
400 g/14 oz spaghetti
4½ cups/1 l/1¾ pt boiling water
salt
a few drops of oil
2 egg yolks
approx. ⅔ cup/100 g/4 oz mascarpone cheese
freshly ground black pepper
60 ml/4 tbsp grated Parmesan cheese

Mascarpone is an Italian cheese sold in muslin (cheesecloth) bags. You can substitute cream cheese if you can't get the real thing.

◆ Hold the spaghetti in a deep pot and pour over the boiling water. Push the spaghetti down into the water. Add more to cover if necessary. Add a pinch of salt and a few drops of oil, cover and cook for 12 minutes. Leave to stand.
◆ Stir the egg yolks into the mascarpone.
◆ Drain the pasta, top with the mascarpone and sprinkle with black pepper and Parmesan.
◆ Heat through for 1 minute, then serve.

PASTA SHELLS WITH CRAB MEAT

SERVES 4 / SET: FULL

Ingredients

3½ cups/400 g/14 oz pasta shells
boiling water
salt
oil
1 scant cup/200 g/7 oz crab meat, flaked
⅔ cup/150 ml/¼ pt single (light) cream
15 ml/1 tbsp marsala
cayenne pepper
chopped parsley

◆ Put the pasta shells in a deep pot, just cover with boiling water, add a pinch of salt and a few drops of oil, cover and cook for 9 minutes. Allow to stand, covered, while you make the sauce.

◆ Stir the crab meat into the cream, add the marsala and cook for 3 minutes.

◆ Drain the pasta, stir in the sauce, sprinkle with cayenne pepper and garnish with chopped parsley.

Pasta shells with crab meat

RIGATONI WITH SARDINES

SERVES 4 / SET: FULL

Ingredients

3½ cups/400 g/14 oz rigatoni

boiling water

salt

15 ml/1 tbsp oil

1 clove garlic, crushed (minced)

scant ¾ cup/125 g/5 oz tinned (canned) sardines in tomato sauce

4 leaves fresh sage, chopped

freshly ground black pepper

◆ Put the rigatoni in a dish and cover with boiling water. Add a pinch of salt and a few drops of the oil, cover and cook for 9 minutes. Leave to stand, covered, while you prepare the sauce.

◆ Put the remaining oil in a bowl and cook for 30 seconds. Add the garlic and cook for 1½ minutes.

◆ Mash the sardines in their tomato sauce and add to the bowl. Cover and cook for 2–3 minutes, stirring once, until hot through.

◆ Drain the pasta, pour the sauce over it, sprinkle with fresh sage and pepper and serve.

PASTA

FRESH VEGETABLES/COOKING GUIDE

vegetables	quantity	minutes on full
globe artichokes	4	10 – 20
asparagus spears	1½ cups/225 g/8 oz	6 – 7
aubergines (eggplant), diced	2 cups/450 g/1 lb	5 – 6
beans, broad (fava, lima), French (green) or runner	2½ cups/450 g/1 lb	8 – 10
beetroot (beets), sliced	4 cups/450 g/1 lb	7 – 8
broccoli florets	6 cups/450 g/1 lb	4 – 5
Brussels sprouts	6 cups/450 g/1 lb	8 – 10
cabbage, shredded	6 cups/450 g/1 lb	7 – 10
carrots, sliced	2 cups/225 g/8 oz	7 – 10
cauliflower florets	6 cups/450 g/1 lb	10 – 11
celery	1 head	10 – 13
corn on the cob	1	3 – 5
courgettes (zucchini), sliced	4	7 – 10
Kohlraki	4 cups/450 g/1 lb	7 – 8
leeks, sliced	4 cups/450 g/1 lb	7 – 10
marrow (squash), sliced	4 cups/450 g/1 lb	8 – 10
mushrooms, whole	2½ cups/225 g/8 oz	5 – 6
okra	4 cups/450 g/1 lb	8 – 10
onions, sliced	2 cups/225 g/8 oz	5 – 7
parsnips, sliced	2 cups/225 g/8 oz	8 – 10
peas	4 cups/450 g/1 lb	7
potatoes, new	6 cups/450 g/1 lb	8 – 10
potatoes, jacket (baked)	2 large	8
potatoes, boiled	4 cups/450 g/1 lb	6 – 7
spinach	2 cups/450 g/1 lb	5
greens, chopped	6 cups/450 g/1 lb	7 – 9
swedes (rutabaga), sliced	3 cups/450 g/1 lb	6 – 7
tomatoes, sliced	1½ cups/450 g/1 lb	2 – 3
turnips, sliced	1½ cups/225 g/8 oz	6 – 7

FROZEN VEGETABLES/COOKING GUIDE

vegetables	quantity	minutes on full
asparagus spears	1½ cups/225 g/8 oz	6 – 7
beans, broad (fava), French (green) or runner	1½ cups/225 g/8 oz	7
broccoli spears	4 cups/225 g/8 oz	6 – 8
cabbage, chopped	3 cups/225 g/8 oz	6 – 7
carrots, sliced	2 cups/225 g/8 oz	6 – 7
cauliflower florets	4 cups/225 g/8 oz	4 – 6
sweetcorn (corn)	2 cups/225 g/8 oz	4 – 6
corn on the cob	1	4 – 5
courgettes (zucchini), sliced	2 cups/225 g/8 oz	4
peas	2 cups/225 g/8 oz	4
spinach, chopped	3 cups/225 g/8 oz	5
swedes (rutabaga), cubed	2 cups/225 g/8 oz	7
turnips, sliced	1½ cups/225 g/8 oz	8
vegetables, mixed	2 cups/225 g/8 oz	4 – 6

FRESH MEAT COOKING GUIDE

meat	minutes on full per 450 g/1 lb	standing minutes
bacon (ham) roast	12 – 14	10
bacon, rashers (slices) 4	4½	—
beef, boned roasts, rare	5 – 6	15 – 20
beef, boneless roast, medium	7 – 8	15 – 20
beef, boneless roast, well-done	8 – 9	15 – 20
beef, roasts with bone, rare	5 – 6	15 – 20
beef, roasts with bone, medium	6 – 7	15 – 20
beef, roasts with bone, well-done	8 – 9	15 – 20
beef, ground, 4 patties	10	5
chicken, whole roast	8 – 10	10 – 15
chicken, portions	6 – 8	10
lamb, boned roast	7 – 8	20
lamb, boned and rolled roast	9	20
lamb, roast with bone	6 – 7	20
lamb, crown roast	9 – 10	20
lamb chops	2	10
liver, ox (beef)	8	5
liver, lamb, calves'	7	5
pork, boned rolled roast	8 – 10	15
pork, roast with bone	8 – 9	15
poussin (Cornish rock hen), pigeon, pheasant, quail	5 – 7	5
sausages (links), 4	4	—
portions	15	10
turkey, whole roast	11	10 – 15

FROZEN MEAT DEFROSTING GUIDE

meat	minutes on low per 450 g/1 lb	standing minutes
beef, boned roasts	8 – 10	30
beef, roasts on bone	8 – 10	30
beef, minced (ground)	8 – 10	2
beef steak, cubed	6 – 8	5
hamburgers, two	2	2
hamburgers, four	4	2
chicken, whole	6 – 8	30
chicken portions	5	30
duck and duckling	5 – 7	30
kidney	6 – 9	5
lamb, boned roasts	5 – 6	30 – 45
lamb, with bone	8 – 10	30 – 45
lamb chops	8 – 10	15
liver	8 – 10	5
pork, boned roasts	7 – 8	30
pork roast with bone	7 – 8	45
poussin (Cornish rock hen), grouse, pigeon, pheasant	5 – 7	10
sausages (links)	5 – 6	5
turkey, whole	10 – 12	60
veal, boned rolled roast	5 – 6	30
veal, with bone	8 – 10	45
veal chops	8 – 10	30
veal, minced (ground)	8 – 10	5

FISH
Defrost and Cooking Guide

fish	weight	defrost minutes	standing minutes	cooking in minutes on full
bass	225 g/8 oz	5 – 6	15	5 – 6
bonito tuna steaks,	225 g/8 oz	10	15	—
bream, sea-bream	225 g/8 oz	—	15	10 – 12
cod fillets	225 g/8 oz	4 – 5	5	4 – 6
cod steaks	225 g/8 oz	5	5	6
crab claws	100 g/4 oz	5	5	2 – 3
crab, dressed (crab cakes)	100 g/4 oz	2	10	—
haddock fillets	100 g/4 oz	4 – 5	5	5 – 7
haddock steaks	100 g/4 oz	4 – 5	5	4 – 7
halibut steaks	100 g/4 oz	4 – 5	5	4 – 5
hake steaks	100 g/4 oz	4 – 5	5	4 – 6
kipper (kippered herrings)	100 g/4 oz	—	—	1 – 2
kipper (kippered herrings) fillets (boil-in-the-bag)	200 g/7 oz	3	5	3
mackerel	225 g/8 oz	6 – 8	8 – 10	4 – 5
mahi-mahi	225 g/8 oz	6 – 8	—	4 – 6
red and grey mullet	225 g/8 oz	6 – 8	8 – 10	4 – 6
mussels	225 g/8 oz	5	5	—
plaice (flounder) fillets	225 g/8 oz	4 – 5	5	4
prawns (small shrimp), cooked	225 g/8 oz	5	5	—
red salmon steaks	225 g/8 oz	5	5	4 – 5
scrod fillets	225 g/8 oz	4 – 5	30	4 – 5
scampi (king prawns), raw		5	5	4 – 6
scallops	225 g/8 oz	5	5	5 – 7
snapper	225 g/8 oz	6 – 8	8 – 10	5 – 7
sole	225 g/8 oz	5 – 6	8 – 10	4
trout	225 g/8 oz	6 – 8	8 – 10	7
yellowtail	225 g/8 oz	6 – 8	8 – 10	7

TIME AND SETTINGS FOR PASTA AND GRAINS

Although there are no real time savings in cooking rice and pasta in the microwave, it may be a more foolproof way of cooking as there is no risk of sticking to the pan. Standing is usually necessary to complete cooking.

Cooking times will vary according to the type of pasta. Fresh pasta needs microwaving for only 1 minute. It requires no standing time, but should just be drained and served immediately. Times for dried pasta and rice are given below.

PASTA AND GRAINS COOKING GUIDE
PER 225 G/8 OZ

food	boiling salted water to add	cooking in minutes on full	standing minutes
long grain rice (1 generous cup)	3 cups/725 ml/1¼ pt	14	5
pudding (Carolina) rice (1 generous cup)	2½ cups/600 ml/1 pt		
American (converted) rice (2½ cups)	2½ cups/600 ml/ 1 pint	12	5
brown rice	3½ cups/900 ml/ 1½ pt	30	5
egg noodles & tagliatelle (fettucini) (6 cups)	4 cups/1 litre/1¾ pt with 2 tsp oil	6 – 8	2 – 3
spaghetti	4 cups/1 litre/1¾ pt with 2 tsp oil	12	5 – 10
pasta shells (2 cups) & shapes	4 cups/1 litre/1¾ pt with 2 tsp oil	12 – 14	5 – 10
macaroni (2 cups)	4 cups/1 litre/1¾ pt with 2 tsp oil	12 – 15	2 – 3
lasagne (6 cups)	4 cups/1 litre/1¾ pt with 2 tsp oil	9	2

CAKES, BREAD AND DESSERTS DEFROSTING GUIDE

product	quantity	minutes on low	standing minutes
bread, whole loaf	1 large	6 – 8	5 – 15
bread, whole loaf	1 small	4 – 6	10
bread, sliced loaf	1 large	6 – 8	10
bread, sliced loaf	1 small	4 – 6	5
bread slice	25 g/1 oz	10 – 15 secs	1 – 2
bread rolls, crumpets, scones (biscuits), etc	2	15 – 20 secs	1 – 2
	4	25 – 35	1 – 2
cakes, cream	2	45 – 60	10
	4	1¼	10
cakes, small	2	30 – 60	5
cupcakes	4	1¼ – 1¾	5
cakes, large:			
sponge (yellow) cake	450 g/1 lb	4	10
cheesecake	23 cm/9 in	3 – 4	20
dough, pizza and bread	450 g/1 lb	4	10
dough, shortcrust and puff	227 g/8 oz	4	20
dough, shortcrust and puff	397 g/14 oz	6	20
mousse (soufflé), small	1	30 secs	15
pie, fruit or cream	650 g/26 oz	5	10
trifle	1	1	15